OVER HONG KONG

Left
Kowloon At the tip of the Kowloon peninsula, the modern hotels, shopping centres and offices of Tsim Sha Tsui East, in the foreground, are built on reclaimed land. On the other side of Chatham Road is the older area of Tsim Sha Tsui.

Right
New Territories Another, quieter side of Hong Kong is seen in the stark beauty of mountains in the New Territories. Some 40% of the territory is designated as country park.

page 8
Hong Kong In this satellite picture of the territory, both the Special Economic Zone of Shenzhen (top left) and Hong Kong's new airport at Chek Lap Kok, off Lantau Island, are clearly seen.

OVER HONG KONG

Photographs by Magnus Bartlett and Kasyan Bartlett

Additional photography by Lew Roberts

Introduction by Nury Vittachi

Preface by Richard Branson

OVER HONG KONG
VOLUME FIVE

Odyssey Books 1998
© Airphoto International Ltd

ISBN 9622175066

Archive acknowledgements:
Landsat TM data acquired & processed by China Remote Sensing Satellite Ground Station.
Distributed by Geocarto International Centre. Copyright © 1997 RSGS China/GIC Hong Kong – page 8
The Hongkong and Shanghai Banking Corporation Limited – page 21
Historic aerials, 1924 and 1945. Source: RAF (UK) – pages 43, 49, 78, 85

All enquiries to:
Pacific Century Publishers Ltd
1003 Kowloon Centre
29-43 Ashley Road, Kowloon, Hong Kong
Tel: 2376 2085 Fax: 2376 2137
E-mail: airman@gateway.net.hk

Colour separation by Daiichi System Graphics Co., Ltd.
Printing by Daiichi Publishers Co., Ltd.
Captions by Hilary Binks and May Holdsworth
Designed by George Ngan

Printed in Hong Kong

Foreword

by Richard Branson

Read the introduction to *Over Hong Kong* and you'll see why, as an independent businessman, I have a very special regard for Hong Kong. In a world continually troubled by recession and economic uncertainty, it has stood out as a supreme example of 'free enterprise in action'. Its people have always been genuine entrepreneurs and born survivors. Its image has always been as one of those rare places where everybody actually enjoys getting things done, and getting them right.

Look through the photographs in *Over Hong Kong* and you'll see why Hong Kong ranks among the world's greatest tourist destinations. Most famously, of course, there are the spectacularly-skyscrapered downtown districts of Hong Kong Island and Kowloon, bracketing the magnificent harbour, with their luxury hotels, and their arcades and streets full of shops and restaurants. Less well-known, but not to be missed, there are the attractions of the open countryside and tranquil beaches waiting to be discovered, beyond the city in the New Territories and Outlying Islands.

Before my first real visit, in November 1993, I had heard at lot about 'The View from the Peak'. Yet nothing could have prepared me for the amazing contrast between what are actually two very different views: on one side, to the north, the panorama of modern Hong Kong in all of its high-rise splendour; on the other, nature pure and simple.

To be in Hong Kong is to sense the intensely exciting workings of a unique city. What has gone on there, and is still going on there today, adds up to an extraordinary modern-day success story; and I, for one, am confident that there are many more chapters of that story still to come.

▌page 10
Wanchai In this 1990 photograph from Airphoto's archives, there is an uncanny similarity between the silhouette of Wanchai and the Manhattan skyline. The former down-market district has sprouted gleaming high-rises, including one of Asia's tallest buildings, the 78-storey Central Plaza.

▌page 11
Victoria Harbour, c. 1989 Hong Kong's sheltered harbour has always been its greatest natural asset. The Kai Tak runway will cease to be operational in 1998 when it is superseded by Hong Kong's new international airport at Chek Lap Kok.

▌Right
Celebration Fireworks In this shot, the roof of Jardine House, rather than a helicopter, offered an unparalleled vantage point from which to view the spectacular firework display held to mark the reunification of Hong Kong with China on 1 July, 1997.

Contents

14

Wanchai The innovative low-rise Hong Kong
Convention & Exhibition Centre is set against a backdrop
of high-rises on the Wanchai waterfront.

pages 14-15
Lantau Link Already a major Hong Kong landmark,
the Tsing Ma Bridge between the islands of Tsing Yi and Ma
Wan is part of the Lantau Link to Hong Kong's new
airport at Chek Lap Kok. A viaduct across Ma Wan
connects with the Kap Shui Bridge to Lantau (left).

Above
Shenzhen The meandering Shenzhen River marks
the boundary between the fishponds of the northern
New Territories of Hong Kong and the Shenzhen Special
Economic Zone.

Right
Ocean Park Situated on a headland overlooking the
East Lamma Channel, Ocean Park is a major recreation
centre which attracts both visitors and locals in their
thousands every year. Aberdeen is in the background.

Introduction

by Nury Vittachi

The poet had gone potty. There was no other explanation for it. Why else would his eyes be shining when the rest of the party could only see windswept coastal scrubland?

Bai Yue-shan, a seer, poet and wizard of the 12th century AD, was with his entourage on a rocky outcrop in the far south of the Middle Kingdom. The San On district of Guangdong Province was a humid, mountainous region, with a scattering of bare islands. A few of these, such as Tai-ki Shan, were lightly populated by fishermen, but that was it. There was nothing at all of interest in this desolate and remote area. Beyond these rocks, there was literally nothing at all — just the Great Sea which went past the lands of the Outer Barbarians to the end of the universe.

Yet the poet's eyes had lit up like beacons. He seemed enraptured by it. "I see a host of stars in the deep night," said Bai. "I see ten thousand ships passing to and fro within the harbour."

One could not blame his followers for having difficulty visualising this. What lay before them were 236 featureless lumps of stone, sparsely covered in vegetation. But the area had its good points. It was rich in wildlife, and scholars had counted 200 species of butterfly. San On was pleasantly temperate during the eighth and ninth moons, so it was said.

Also, there was a bay on the other side of one of the main islands from which it was said you could smell the perfume of flowers and spices, when you were many leagues out at sea. Merchant sailors named the place Heung Gong, which could be translated as Perfumed Bay, or Fragrant Harbour. (The Outer Barbarians referred to the district as The Ladrones, which was Portuguese for "The Pirate Islands".)

You could certainly see the cooking fires of the fishing boats when dusk fell — but a host of stars shining from the island? You would need a lot of imagination. Bai Yue-shan's comments were duly recorded and filed, and the area sank into tranquil obscurity for the next few centuries.

History is generally seen as a river, a flowing channel that shapes the lives of the people along its banks. But Hong Kong's history is markedly different. It has always moved in sharply defined, abrupt steps, some of which can be marked to a particular day, hour, or even minute. Even more interesting, the stages of this development are still visible to the educated eye, and can be quite clearly seen in the photographs of this book. Don the mantle of an armchair archaeologist, and you can find, in this volume, the individual strata of one of the world's strangest historical anomalies.

The rolling hills that Bai Yue-shan's followers saw are still clearly visible. Some 80 per cent of the 1,092 square kilometre territory of Hong Kong remains rural. Half of this greenery has been protected by law since the 1970s as official country parks, where no development is allowed. The common image of Hong Kong as a city of narrow streets and shoulder-to-shoulder buildings is as inaccurate today as it has always been.

Left
Hong Kong Convention & Exhibition Centre
A pleasing diversity of modern architectural styles is seen in Wanchai, the sweeping low-rise Convention Centre extension contrasting with the soaring spire of Central Plaza on the right.

| Left
Hong Kong Island From its very beginning, Hong Kong's developers have sought space on the waterfront. As a result, reclamation has forced the shoreline outwards into the harbour.

| Above
Hong Kong Island, c. 1880 The profile of Hong Kong Island looked very different 120 years ago. The great hongs like Dent & Co. and Jardine, Matheson & Co. built their godowns along the Central Praya and the thriving town of Victoria sprang up behind. Below the Botanical Gardens, Government House then enjoyed an unobstructed view of Kowloon. The Gothic tower of St John's Cathedral still stands today, now dwarfed by skyscrapers.

But Bai's vision, the city which looked like a galaxy of stars, has also become clearly visible, particularly in pictures of Hong Kong at night. In between, there have been several other fascinating stages, and all of these can still be seen, too. Let us look at the most discussed step in the development of Hong Kong. If its long pre-history as a low-traffic fishing village was Phase One, then we can use the term Phase Two to describe the British colonial era.

One January morning in 1841, the fishermen of Tai-ki Shan noticed that a group of Outer Barbarians had landed. They had seen Westerners before, but usually they were on their way up the Pearl River estuary to the city of Guangzhou, which foreigners called Canton (a mis-pronunciation of the Chinese province name, Guangdong).

Sunburned, sweaty and over-dressed, the Outer Barbarians set up shop on the island. The British Government sent a series of 28 governors to look after the fast-expanding settlement, some of whom were even more odd than the first arrivees. There was Sir Samuel Bonham of 1848, for example, who started a tradition of the most senior Barbarian wearing a funny hat with white feathers springing from the top.

During this phase, this corner of the Celestial Kingdom grew to a major transshipment centre and a thriving port city. During the reign of Sir Reginald Stubbs, 1919-1925, a famous visitor dropped by: Dr Sun Yat-sen, called the father of modern China, visited the colony and was highly impressed by what he saw. "I began to wonder how it was that foreigners, that Englishmen, could do such things... with the barren rock of Hong Kong within 70 or 80 years, while China, in 4,000 years, had no place like Hong Kong," said the Chinese leader.

Much of this book is filled with the evidence of the growth during the British era: the urbanisation that grew at immense speed, the creation of towns that today still exist under the same historical names of Causeway Bay, Victoria Peak and Prince Edward. Some of the original buildings of the early decades are still visible, such as Government House, and St John's Cathedral. Even Hong Kong's best known transport systems are still running routes chosen 100 years ago. The Peak Tram was opened in 1888, and the Star Ferry first crossed the harbour from Hong Kong Island to Kowloon in 1898.

When did the British era finish? June 30, 1997, right? Wrong. If you take the politics out of Hong Kong history and look at it from the point of view of society and economics, you get a different story. It is arguable that Hong Kong was really a British colony for only about 120 years. One day in 1958, at the beginning of the reign of Sir Robert Black, an extraordinary memo arrived from London. It said that the UK Government no longer felt the need to oversee Hong Kong finances.

From that day on, the Budget was handled by the Hong Kong Government alone. That may well be the day this place really stopped being a colony. Let us call this Phase Three, a period in which Hong Kong transcended its colonial status.

In the 1960s and 1970s, the city acquired a unique and independent character as an efficient, lightly governed, super-productive centre, with growing business connections with Shenzhen.

In the 1980s, the British phrase "Crown Colony" almost completely vanished, to be replaced with "territory". The main island of Hong Kong, formerly called Victoria, was silently renamed "Hong Kong Island" by common but unspoken consent. By the 1990s, the cognoscenti realised that a massive change had taken place, but the Hong Kong administration could find no way to announce it that would accord with political protocol.

So it was announced with silence. When the 150th anniversary of the founding of the Crown Colony of Hong Kong came around, in January, 1991, the date was not marked in any way. No celebrations, no fireworks, not a single official statement. The wordless message was as loud as a foghorn. We are not a colony now, and hope not to be, ever again.

This phase of Hong Kong's history is when the city changed from being an Asian industrial city not unlike Kuala Lumpur or Jakarta into the spectacular and futuristic cityscape it is today.

In Phase Three, Hong Kong became wealthier than the UK. It ended the period with HK$500 billion (that's not a misprint) in its savings account. The wealth and architectural exuberance of that era is much in evidence in this book. A quintessential example is Shatin, which grew in less than 20 years from poor farmland (Shatin is Cantonese for "sandy field") to a massive satellite city-within-a-city.

But you can see this growth on many pages of this book: sprawling urban developments piling up like

snowdrift in the foothills of the mountains; a new airport, one of the world's biggest, taking shape in the sea; high-speed land reclamation turning the central harbour into a meandering river; a new bridge which looks like a concrete giant using tiny Ma Wan Island as a stepping stone to Lantau Island; and buildings so high their upper floors are lost in the clouds.

The platform on which the new Hong Kong airport is being built, beautifully captured in these pages, has been declared the biggest building site in the world. But when you look at the other reclamations, such as the expansion of West Kowloon, you realise that term could apply to the territory as a whole.

The growth of frenetic activity is not just on land. At the turn of the century, about 11,000 small ships berthed in Hong Kong each year. Today, it is one of the world's busiest ports, with 82,000 huge boats arriving each year, carrying 125 million tonnes of cargo.

Political maturity arrived at the end of this phase. After public consultations, the 28th and last Governor, Christopher Patten (1992-1997), decided that Hong Kong people should be given an elected parliament and full British passports. The foreign ministries of both China and Britain were horrified at this, and the result was energetic and widespread political discussion in Hong Kong for the first time.

Now we have just entered the Fourth Phase — the most nervously anticipated stage of all: post-handover "Hong Kong, China". Of course, it is too early to see the effects of this largely political change in the architecture of the city. But this may change.

The Beijing-appointed chief executive, Tung Chee-hwa, has ominously said that he does not consider the protected parks inviolable. He has also made it clear that he plans to move fast with massive construction plans. These two facts mean that some of the green in this book may not be there in future editions.

People from a business background sometimes fail to realise that growth of urbanisation is not good news,

Right
Hong Kong Island The density of building in Central district extends up the hillsides to the residential towers of Mid Levels, putting great strain on basic aspects of the infrastructure such as transport and sewage systems.

Far left
Yau Ma Tei This historical picture taken in the late 1980s shows the old Yau Ma Tei typhoon shelter, which provided refuge for all manner of craft from tiny sampans to large fishing boats and lighters, on the west side of the Kowloon peninsula. It has since been filled in to create much-needed new land for the expansion of Kowloon.

Left
West Kowloon Reclamation A major function of the massive new West Kowloon Reclamation is to provide land for the West Kowloon Expressway, part of the transport network leading to Chek Lap Kok. Here both new rail and road tunnels emerge from Hong Kong Island. A new Yau Ma Tei typhoon shelter has been created further west (right).

per se. A labyrinth of arcane land use and inheritance laws in the New Territories has meant that Hong Kong's "green lung" has regularly been attacked by developers bent on short-term profit. Pictures of the Mai Po Marshes, a preserved area of tropical wetland, now show it next to a huge, web-shaped private housing development.

The photographers who have been taking these photographs for more than a decade note a remarkable drop in the number of days when the air has that crystal-clear quality associated with less spoiled parts of Asia. One is reminded of those lines from Shakespeare's *Hamlet*: "This most excellent canopy the air, look you, this brave o'er-hanging firmament, this majestical roof fretted with golden fire – why, it appeareth no other thing to me than a foul and pestilent congregation of vapours."

But there has been a growing awareness of environmental issues in Hong Kong over the past decade. Campaigners are hoping the new administration will realise it has the opportunity to guide development into more traditional Chinese lines, where harmony between man and nature is seen as the cornerstone of a civilised society. At the brink of the third millennium, Hong Kong is one of the few cities in Asia which has the wealth, both intellectual and fiscal, to mould itself into a role model for fast-developing China.

Hong Kong has more green "escapes" for its residents than probably any major city in the world. These have been retained without any major hindrance to economic growth. Here is a model for the world, if only people in power will heed it.

This book helps. It reminds us that the oft-photographed Hong Kong Island adds up to less than a tenth of the 1,092 sq kilometres of the territory. It surprises us, too. Often, the most memorable sights from an aerial view are the most ordinary to local people on the ground: the boats that people here use as daily public transport; the airport runway that juts into the sea like a road to nowhere; the curious geometric patterns of building developments; the fish farms, the typhoon shelters, and so on.

The book's aerial view also places dramatically contrasting aspects of Hong Kong's multiple personality side by side. Aberdeen's floating village is populated by families on old, wooden boats, who are in some ways the spiritual descendants of the Tanka people who were in Hong Kong before it became a British colony. Yet towering over the boats are the gleaming towers of South Horizon, a huge complex of modern white skyscrapers, with each tiny flat now worth more than a typical house in London.

If you arrive in Hong Kong on a night flight to Kai Tak, the city is a visionary, neon-lit metropolis from the future. But trip down the back alleys the following morning, and you find a place of temples and ancient magic. A form of Chinese geomancy called *fung shui* (literally "wind-water") pervades the lives of even the most serious and businesslike people here.

A mystical vortex of negative power is widely believed to exist in the garden of Government House, which allegedly receives bad vibrations from the Bank of China Building. This skyscraper, one of the tallest buildings in Asia, is made up of a network of interlocking triangles. In *fung shui*, it is held that a sharp angle pointing at you

Right
Fairview Park Surrounded by the Mai Po Marshes Nature Reserve, Fairview Park is a middle-class housing development in the northwest New Territories which offers low-rise living and recreational facilities.

focuses bad forces in your direction.

Hong Kong's new leader, businessman Tung Chee-hwa, has steadfastly refused to move into the residence, despite its being palatial, conveniently situtated, and ideally designed for a head of state. He has not admitted that it is because of the bad vibrations, but local people have taken it for granted.

For the British, midnight on June 30, 1997 was much more than just the handover of one small settlement. After all, Hong Kong is a tiny patch of the world. But the ceremony marked the end of Britain's great colonial adventure of the past two centuries. The end of the Empire.

True, there are still several other British colonies around the world, Gibraltar and the Falkland Islands being the best known. But none have the strange history and visual drama of Hong Kong, a society of six million chopstick-favouring Chinese souls right on the edge of mainland China, until this year ruled over by knife-and-fork wielding Oxbridge graduates from 6,000 miles away.

At the moment Prince Charles watched the Union flag flutter downwards, at 11.59 pm on June 30, 1997, the Hong Kong of the *gwailo*, the ghost people, vanished. The city-state became Xianggang, a region of China.

And tonight, as every night, the darkness will fall, and the city will turn into China's galaxy of stars, twinkling in the night over a harbour full of ships.

Somewhere, the ghost of a man named Bai Yue-shan smiles and bows.

Right
Victoria Harbour On either side of Hong Kong's spectacular natural harbour, the population of six and a half million is concentrated in the urban areas. The Kowloon hills rise in the distance.

▌Left
Chek Lap Kok and Tung Chung In the late 1980s, after an extensive study, the island of Chek Lap Kok off the northwest coast of Lantau Island was chosen as the site for Hong Kong's new international airport. The Tung Chung Valley in the foreground was also earmarked for development as Hong Kong's ninth new town, the first on an outlying island. At the time, Chek Lap Kok was uninhabited and Tung Chung was a small coastal village accessible only by sea.

▌Above
Chek Lap Kok Just 28 kilometres from the heart of Hong Kong, the 1,248-hectare airport site at Chek Lap Kok is now the size of the Kowloon peninsula and four times larger than the existing airport at Kai Tak. It remains separated from Lantau Island by a narrow water channel. The new town of Tung Chung will house a population of 200,000 by the year 2011.

▌Above
Chek Lap Kok Chek Lap Kok is seen here in the early stages of construction. By levelling Chek Lap Kok Island and reclaiming land from the sea, a platform was formed for Hong Kong's new airport in one of the most challenging civil engineering projects in the world today. A transport network of roads and railway has been built to link the new airport with the urban areas of Hong Kong Island and Kowloon.

▌Right
Chek Lap Kok Designed by Sir Norman Foster, the Chek Lap Kok passenger terminal and Y-shaped concourse is 1.2 kilometres long and covers an area of 490,000 square metres. The terminal will have the capability to process 35 million passengers annually. On opening, the airport will have one runway operating around the clock. A second runway will follow to meet future demand.

▌Following page
Sunset Peak, Lantau Island Close to the summit of Sunset Peak, a series of curious stone huts are dotted either side of the path. Some belong to local religious organizations, while others are privately owned. It is said that during the Japanese occupation of Hong Kong during World War II, British officers and escaped prisoners used these huts as hide-outs.

THE ISLAND

Page 33
Western Approaches A jetcat follows a jetfoil in through the Western approaches of Victoria Harbour, towards the Macau Ferry Pier in front of the red and black Shun Tak Centre. A number of services operate regularly from Hong Kong to the Portuguese enclave 65 kilometres away across the Pearl River Estuary, including jetfoils, jetcats, high-speed ferries and even a helicopter. Green Island, on the right, was originally used as a magazine, and then as a holding point for illegal Vietnamese immigrants in the 1980s. It will eventually cease to be an island when it is swallowed up by further reclamation.

Left
Western District Once one of the oldest and most traditional areas of Hong Kong, Western has been transformed by steel and glass high-rise development over the past decade as rents skyrocket in Central District beyond. New roads intertwine towards the entrance to the new Western Harbour Tunnel, opened in 1997, which will ease congestion at the other two harbour crossings. The two-kilometre, six-lane road tunnel from Sai Ying Pun connects to the southern end of the West Kowloon Expressway leading to Hong Kong's new airport at Chek Lap Kok. The low grey building in the foreground is the Hongkong Tramways terminal, with Western wholesale market close to the shore.

Above
North Shore, Hong Kong Island Seen from above Tsim Sha Tsui, Kowloon, the north shore of Hong Kong Island from Wanchai to Kennedy Town rises spectacularly against the backdrop of Victoria Peak, often overhung by cloud. The development of this inhospitable terrain is a triumph of architectural engineering, with buildings constructed on reclamation or clinging to the mountainside, in an attempt to meet Hong Kong's insatiable appetite for economic growth. The new Airport Railway to Chek Lap Kok, travelling from its terminus on the Central Reclamation, will emerge on the West Kowloon Reclamation (right), while the Cross-Harbour road tunnel from Western also surfaces close by.

Above
Central District Taken from a light aircraft, this photograph dating from the early 1980s illustrates the incredible growth which has occurred along the Central waterfront over the past 15 years. The twin arms of the Star Ferry pier have survived but L-shaped Blake Pier has been swallowed up by reclamation. Here the pink towers of Exchange Square are just under construction to the right of portholed Connaught Centre (now Jardine House). The Hong Kong Land Company paid HK$4,755 million for the 13,400 square metre site, making it the most expensive site in the world at that time.

Right
Central Reclamation Part of a reclamation plan for the whole north shore of Hong Kong Island, the first 20-hectare phase in Central will provide land for the expansion of Central and the terminus for the new Airport Railway to Chek Lap Kok. This will be an express service, stopping only at West Kowloon and Tsing Yi as it whisks travellers from Central to the airport in a little over 20 minutes. The construction project was complicated by the need to move the Outlying Islands ferry piers out from the old shoreline while still keeping them in operation. The latest architectural landmark in Central is the Land Development Corporation's 73-storey Jubilee Street project.

▌Above
Admiralty and Central District In 1982, the naval basin of H.M.S. Tamar, the former headquarters of the British Forces in Hong Kong, was still in full operation, playing host to both British Naval vessels and visiting war ships from other countries. The black towers of Admiralty stand behind the patrol craft, next to the gold Far East Finance Centre, while further to the right the Hilton (now demolished), Furama and Mandarin Hotels are visible. The open space to the left of Admiralty was soon to be developed into Pacific Place. In those days, Connaught Centre (now Jardine House) behind the Star Ferry pier was unmatched in height in Central. To the right of the Hilton, red cranes mark the site of the new Hongkong Bank headquarters under construction.

▌Right
Central District The financial and business heart of Hong Kong occupies barely a square kilometre, its towers reaching skywards from incredibly small sites. The pink towers on the left are Exchange Square, home of the Hong Kong Stock Exchange, beside portholed Jardine House. In between that and the twin white towers of the Landmark office and shopping complex, is Swire House, soon to be demolished and rebuilt. Dominating the banks is I.M. Pei's pyramidal Bank of China, with the dark towers of Citybank Plaza to its right. In front of that, St. John's Cathedral is one of Hong Kong's oldest buildings, consecrated in 1849. On the right, after 150 years of British rule, the red flag of the Hong Kong Special Administrative Region now flies from Government House.

▌Above
Victoria Harbour In the early 1980s, Hong Kong's harbour was much wider than it is today. Since then the territory's population has risen from 5.2 million to 6.3 million, making the creation of more land necessary. On the other hand, whereas only 22,000 ocean-going vessels visited Hong Kong every year in those days, now the figure is close to 83,000, in a much-reduced harbour. One reason for lack of space on the Kowloon peninsula, which has led to extensive reclamation, was the height restriction imposed to clear the flight path to Kai Tak Airport (top left). With the opening of Hong Kong's new airport at Chek Lap Kok, this has been lifted.

▌Right
Victoria Harbour With its land area of only 1,092 square kilometres and a population of almost six and a half million, Hong Kong is one of the most densely populated places in the world. The situation is exacerbated by the fact that most of the population is concentrated in the urban areas: Hong Kong Island and Kowloon have an average of more than 26,000 people per square kilometre. Many of the buildings rising cheek by jowl in this 1996 photograph are already built on reclaimed land, yet still more reclamation is in progress. Public concern is now growing that this kind of rampant intrusion into Victoria Harbour might end up jeopardizing Hong Kong's greatest natural asset.

Left
Tamar This large, temporarily open area to the east of Central is the recently reclaimed old H.M.S. Tamar British naval base, once home of the Hong Kong Squadron. The British Navy had a presence in Hong Kong from 1841 until their departure in the early hours of 1st July 1997. Appropriately, the site was used for the official ceremony on 30th June 1997 to mark the end of British administration in Hong Kong. The area is now earmarked for a new Government headquarters. The building on the left is CITIC Tower. The one on the right was formerly the Prince of Wales Building, Headquarters of British Forces in Hong Kong, and is now the Headquarters of the People's Liberation Army in the territory.

Right
H.M.S. Tamar In 1945 the Royal Air Force began regular aerial survey missions of Hong Kong and this is one of the results. It is interesting to see how flat the city appears, with no high-rise buildings. There is noticeably much less shipping in the harbour than today. The vessels at anchor are probably warships and there are also naval vessels moored at H.M.S. Tamar.

Following pages
Victoria Peak In the 19th century, the Peak was an exclusive retreat of wealthy taipans and still remains a smart residential area for Hong Kong's richest and most influential inhabitants. Today the stately colonial residences with their lawns and pools are outnumbered by modern townhouses. In 1996 more than one million visitors made their way to the Peak for stunning views of the harbour and outlying islands. Many came by the Peak Tram, actually a funicular railway, which rises 373 metres on a gradient as steep as one-in-two from Garden Road in Central to Victoria Gap, 397 metres above sea level. The Peak Tram began operating in 1888 and is Hong Kong's oldest public transport.

Above
Central, 1983 "Betsy", the original DC-3 aircraft purchased by Cathay Pacific Airways in 1946, returned home to Hong Kong in March 1983. Here she is seen flying past the site of the new extension to the Hong Kong Convention & Exhibition Centre. Wanchai Sports Ground on the left remains today, but the Wanchai waterfront has changed perhaps more dramatically than any other part of Hong Kong Island in the last decade. Note that in those days, the circular Hopewell Centre towered above Wanchai, whereas now Central Plaza dominates.

Right
Hong Kong Convention and Exhibition Centre
Hong Kong's newest and most exciting architectural achievement, the extension to the Hong Kong Convention and Exhibition Centre sits on an artificial island that juts into the harbour on the Wanchai waterfront, providing possibly the most magnificent setting for a convention centre anywhere in the world. Images of the centre were beamed to television viewers worldwide on 30th June 1997 when it was the scene of the historic handover ceremony between Britain and China. Symbolising a sea bird soaring into flight, the building features a 40,000-square-metre sculpted aluminium roof, the largest in the world.

Left

Causeway Bay From Causeway Bay in the foreground to Western district at the far right, the north shore of Hong Kong Island is now a continuous ribbon of development, silhouetted against Mount Nicholson, Mount Cameron and Victoria Peak. It was in Causeway Bay that the famous hong, Jardine Matheson and Company Limited was established in 1841. The Jardine's Noon Day Gun, immortalised by Noel Coward in his song, "Mad Dogs and Englishmen", is situated in a garden opposite the Excelsior Hotel (the white building on the left). It is still fired every day on the stroke of midday and on special occasions.

Right

Wanchai, 1945 By 1945, when this photograph was taken, a considerable amount of reclamation had already taken place along the north shore of Hong Kong Island. Here new land has been created in Wanchai, to the east of the H.M.S. Tamar basin. Being newly reclaimed, it was possible to layout the streets in a geometrical pattern, in contrast with the higgledy-piggledy streets of older areas of Hong Kong. Note that in those days Gloucester Road ran along the waterfront. The aircraft carrier at lower left is probably H.M.S. Indomitable, the flagship of the British fleet which entered the harbour to mark the liberation of Hong Kong.

▌Above
Wanchai, c.1982 Extensive reclamation work in the
early 1980s was changing the profile of the Wanchai
waterfront still further. The skyscrapers on the south side
of the waterfront Gloucester Road, which then looked
across to Kowloon with an unobstructed view, now face
others equally high on the other side of the road. Amongst
the first of these were Telecom House and, behind it, the
Hong Kong Arts Centre, built in 1972. Many of the
buildings to the south of Gloucester Road are still
recognizable today.

▌Right
Causeway Bay Bordered by Wanchai to the west,
Causeway Bay is a prime shopping, hotel and
entertainment mecca on Hong Kong Island, boasting
numerous Japanese department stores and shopping malls
as well as street markets and restaurants. The "Bay", once
a natural feature of the island's intricate coastline, has long
since been swallowed up by reclamation. Hennessy Road,
named after a former governor of Hong Kong, is the main
artery running east-west. As well as cars and buses, it
carries the famous system of trams which have trundled
along Hong Kong Island's north shore since 1904.

Left
Causeway Bay Typhoon Shelter When a typhoon threatens during the May-October season, this shelter and others like it around the territory's coastline are crammed full of junks, lighters, sampans and other craft seeking sanctuary. At other times, the shelter is home to a wide spectrum of boats - from simple working sampans close to the shore to gleaming luxury motor yachts inside the sea wall. On the left is the Island Eastern Corridor, built in the 1980s to relieve congestion in the densely populated areas of north Hong Kong Island and to provide speedy access to the eastern end of the Island. The pleasant green area of Victoria Park is on the left.

Above
Victoria Park Thousands of supporters gathered to form a symbolic footprint in Victoria Park on 1st September 1996, marking the start of a charity walk to Beijing. Hong Kong big business is not only self-seeking, as some may think, but is well known for its philanthropy. Every year, thanks to the generosity of both private citizens and corporations, the Community Chest is able to support countless different charitable causes in the territory, while the per capita contribution to charity in Hong Kong is one of the highest in the world.

▌Left

Causeway Bay Next to the Causeway Bay typhoon shelter, traffic pours into the Hong Kong entrance of the Cross-Harbour Tunnel. Until this first tunnel was built in 1972, the only way to cross Victoria Harbour from Hong Kong Island to Kowloon was by ferry. In 1989 a second tunnel, the Eastern Harbour Tunnel, was built linking Quarry Bay and Cha Kwo Ling, and in April 1997 a third, the Western Harbour Tunnel, opened between Sai Ying Pun and the West Kowloon Reclamation. Nevertheless, this tunnel still carries a daily average of 124,000 vehicles. To the left of the tunnel entrance is the Police Officers' Club. In the left background the Hong Kong Stadium hosts the annual Rugby Sevens tournament.

▌Above

Royal Hong Kong Yacht Club Despite the change of sovereignty, members of the Royal Hong Kong Yacht Club (right) decided not to give up the colonial prefix to their club's name. Originally an island, the club's premises are now connected to the north shore of Hong Kong Island by reclamation, with moorings for hundreds of yachts and pleasure craft in the adjacent typhoon shelter. West of the club is the Wanchai public cargo handling area, where goods from vessels moored in the harbour are brought ashore by barge for onward shipment by road. On the left, the Wanchai Sports Ground is a popular venue for athletic events.

▌Left
Happy Valley Between Wanchai and Causeway Bay is Happy Valley, home to Hong Kong's oldest horseracing venue. The first races were held in Happy Valley in 1846 on land reclaimed from a malaria-ridden swamp. Today the stands are packed every Wednesday evening during the season from September to May. Horseracing is the territory's only legal form of gambling and Hong Kong's most popular spectator sport. Saturday meetings are also held, at the Hong Kong Jockey Club's other racecourse in Shatin, New Territories. A percentage of the billions of dollars wagered is given to charity, making the Jockey Club one of the territory's most generous benefactors.

▌Above
Quarry Bay The oldest industrial area in Hong Kong, Quarry Bay has taken off in recent years as soaring land values have made rentals in Central prohibitive. Shipbuilding began in Quarry Bay with the establishment of the Whampoa Dock in 1863. By 1908 the Taikoo Dockyard, founded by Butterfield & Swire, was in full operation and later the Taikoo sugar refinery was built. In the early 1970s, however, the docklands were filled in to make way for the 60 residential towers of Taikoo Shing (left). The refinery and industrial buildings around it gave way to high-rise offices such as the black and white towers of Taikoo Place. Mount Parker rises on the right; the Shaukeiwan typhoon shelter and Chai Wan are in the background.

▌Left
Shek O Country Club On the wild southeast coastline of Hong Kong Island, the Shek O Country Club is possibly the most exclusive club in Hong Kong, with membership highly sought after. When the club was founded in 1921, there was no road to Shek O. Until one was built in 1923, members travelled by boat to Stanley and proceeded from there to the club on foot or on horseback. Overlooking the glorious 18-hole seaside golf course are some of the most spacious and luxurious mansions in the territory, traditionally occupied by Hong Kong taipans. Above Big Wave Bay, a favourite surfers' haunt, loom the ruggedly beautiful Mount Collinson and Pottinger Peak, with Mount Parker behind.

▌Above
Shek O The village of Shek O is a charming blend of contrasts and incongruities. Plush residences on the headland of the peninsula contrast sharply with the slightly shabby original village, populated by a mixture of older villagers and fisherfolk, Chinese commuters and a growing number of trendy expatriates. The village boasts a small Tin Hau temple, a square where villagers sit and talk, a Thai restaurant, and Chinese-style houses either side of narrow alleyways. Shek O is less accessible than most places on Hong Kong Island, leaving its sandy beaches largely deserted during the week. The red-roofed clubhouse of the Shek O Country Club is seen at right. Stanley Peninsula appears beyond the ridge, with Lamma Island in the distance.

Left
Redhill Much controversy surrounded the construction of this enormous luxury residential development in the 1980s, with environmentalists denouncing the desecration of a once beautiful and secluded peninsula. Sadly, residential architecture is often less imaginative than commercial building in Hong Kong. Across Turtle Cove the Stanley Peninsula extends into the East Lamma Channel, the main deep sea entrance for shipping approaching Hong Kong. Bluff Head, at its tip, is the southernmost point of Hong Kong Island. The Hong Kong International School, one of the network of American Schools established worldwide, is in the right foreground.

Above
Tai Tam Opened in 1987, the Country Club facility of the American Club offers members a unique alternative venue for relaxation that complements the Town Club in Exchange Square, Central. It is also especially convenient for the many American families who live in the Manhattan and Pacific View apartments close by. To the right is Tai Tam Tuk Reservoir, built to meet the demands of the growing early population of the territory. Today, most of Hong Kong's water supply is brought in from the mainland by pipeline. The surrounding Tai Tam Country Park is the largest country park on Hong Kong Island, providing miles of hiking trails, picnic spots and spectacular mountain and coastal views.

▌Above

Stanley In 1841 when the British founded the colony of Hong Kong, Stanley was the island's largest village, with a population of 2,000 residents, mostly fishermen. In those days it was also notorious for its pirates and smuggling activities. In fact, its name in the Hakka dialect, Chek Chue, means "robbers' lair" and the pirate Cheung Po Tsai is said to have donated a bell and drum to the local Tin Hau temple. The large under-developed area at the southern end of the peninsula is Stanley Fort, a military base once occupied by the British garrison and now home to a contingent of PLA forces. At the extreme tip of the headland is Hong Kong Telecom's satellite earth station. Po Toi and Beaufort Islands are on the left, the Lema Islands in the distance.

▌Right

Stanley Stanley Prison must enjoy one of the most scenic locations of any correctional institution in the world, perched on the edge of the Stanley Peninsula overlooking the South China Sea. Stanley was the scene of heroic resistance to the Japanese invasion of Hong Kong in 1941 and many Hong Kong civilians spent the next four years interned in a camp on what is now the prison site until the Japanese surrender in August 1945. To the left of the prison a huge underground sewage treatment plant has been constructed in a cavern beneath the hillside. In the centre, the red-roofed building is St. Stephen's College, a leading Hong Kong school. On a clear day like this, it is possible to see as far as Discovery Bay, Lantau (top left) and Tsuen Wan, New Territories (top centre).

Above

Stanley Today, the village of Stanley, nestling picturesquely on the sandbar at the beginning of the Stanley Peninsula, is best known for its market which specializes in clothing, jewellery and Chinese handicrafts. Coach parties of visitors from all over the world flock to Stanley in search of bargains, although in recent years prices and the quality of goods have risen somewhat and the narrow pedestrian streets have been smartened up. Lamma Island with its coal-fired power station, quarry and seafood restaurants can be seen in the background. The narrowness of the East Lamma Channel at this point requires careful navigation and all shipping is in the control of the port authorities.

Right

Stanley Beach Windsurfing has become very popular among young people in Hong Kong in recent years. Stanley is a leading venue for the sport, having the advantages of easy access to its sandy beach, clean and sheltered water, and unimpeded winds. Local enthusiasm for this energetic pursuit was further fuelled by the recent success of Hong Kong athlete Lee Lai-shan, who became the first Hong Kong Olympic Gold Medal winner in history at the Atlanta Games in 1996. Windsurfers are stored on racks at the back of the beach ready for a quick getaway after work in the evenings or at weekends.

▌Left
Chung Hom Kok Chung Hom Kok was one of the
first areas to be developed for luxury residential
accommodation on the south side of Hong Kong Island.
Residents appreciate the low-rise, peaceful environment, the
village atmosphere, stunning location and sea views, as well
as their own secluded sandy beach (right). Commuters may
drive or take a bus to Central District in about half an hour.
To the left, the Ma Hang Village development has replaced
an old squatter settlement and provides low-cost
government housing for several thousand people. Stanley
Village and the Stanley Peninsula are in the background.

▌Above
South Side, Hong Kong Island Unlike the north
shore of Hong Kong Island, whose profile has been altered
by a series of reclamations, the south side has remained
mercifully untouched. One glorious sandy bay succeeds
another on this greener coastline, surmounted by
upmarket residential complexes and country parkland.
Ocean Park (right) perches on the headland above Deep
Water Bay with its yacht anchorage at Middle Island.
Beyond Repulse Bay in the centre, the Chung Hom Kok
and Stanley Peninsulas extend into the South China Sea,
with the deep inlet of Tai Tam Bay further east.

▌ Above

▌South Bay Before the first road was built across the island in 1920, the south side was an area of tropical vegetation where wild game roamed, quite inaccessible except by sedan chairs carried by coolies over rough tracks. Ever since, those seeking peace away from the busy north shore have built houses along this coast, which has often been called Hong Kong's Riviera. South Bay (right) and Middle Bay (left) have two of the island's pleasantest beaches, especially in winter when the crowds have departed. There are 41 gazetted bathing beaches in Hong Kong - 12 on Hong Kong Island and 29 in the New Territories and Outlying Islands - equipped with changing facilities and supervised by lifeguards during the summer. Water quality is also now monitored for pollution.

▌ Right

▌Repulse Bay Sheltered and shallow, beautiful Repulse Bay got its name from a 19th-century pirate chaser, the H.M.S. Repulse, which once patrolled the area. Today, thousands of bathers and sun-worshippers flock to Hong Kong Island's most popular beach on summer weekends. So great has the demand for space become that the beach was recently more than doubled in size by a vast import of sand from the mainland. Repulse Bay is a much favoured residential area and every possible square foot of seafront space is gradually becoming occupied by highrises or town houses. The popular Chinese-style Lido development at the eastern end of the beach has two large statues of the deities Kwun Yum and Tin Hau, both protectors of fishermen.

▌Left
Repulse Bay Repulse Bay used to be famous for its luxury hotel of the same name, built in 1920. The Repulse Bay Hotel became a favourite haunt of the rich and famous, including many well-known film stars. The classic movie "Love is a Many Splendoured Thing" starring Jennifer Jones and William Holden was filmed here. In 1982 Hongkong & Shanghai Hotels tore down the hotel to make way for a high-rise development. In accordance with ancient *fung shui* beliefs, this was built with a hole to allow the local dragon free access from the mountain to the sea. Such was the public outcry at the loss of the hotel that a replica was built on the site of the original.

▌Above
Middle Island Between Deep Water Bay and Repulse Bay (centre left) a small steep islet, Middle Island, lies just offshore, creating a picturesque little lagoon where yachts, junks and other smaller craft lie moored. Both the Royal Hong Kong Yacht Club and the Aberdeen Boat Club have moorings and club facilities at Middle Island, which has become a popular centre for dinghy sailing. A scenic promenade skirts the lagoon, providing a pleasant walk, jog or roller blading circuit between the two bays. Above it luxury residences nestle in the low, green, wooded slopes.

Ocean Park Spectacularly situated on a high promontory between Aberdeen and Deep Water Bay, 87-hectare Ocean Park is Hong Kong's premier park for recreation, boasting Southeast Asia's largest oceanarium. Over 3.5 million people visited Ocean Park in 1995/6 and the park has received more than 40 million visitors since it was originally opened with Hong Kong Jockey Club funding in 1977. Besides entertainment, Ocean Park also has a more serious role: in 1996 the Ocean Park Conservation Foundation was set up to coordinate regional efforts in the conservation of endangered whales and dolphins. Access to the headland is either by the world's longest outdoor escalator, seen here rising from Aberdeen, or by cablecar from the other side of the hill.

Right
Ocean Park Among Ocean Park's varied attractions on the headland are world-class exhibits such as the Atoll Reef, Wave Cove, Shark Aquarium, Bird Paradise, the Butterfly House, and the 3,500-seat Ocean Theatre for marine mammal shows, together with an exciting array of thrill rides. Riding the gigantic "Dragon" rollercoaster, one feels certain to fly right off the headland into the South China Sea, before plunging back inland in dizzying swoops and turns.

▌Above
Shouson Hill The residential area of Shouson Hill, near Aberdeen, is named after Sir Shouson Chow, the first Chinese to be appointed to the Executive Council in 1926. Access from Central was greatly facilitated in 1982 by the opening of the Aberdeen Tunnel (left, foreground), which links the north and south sides of Hong Kong Island. Measuring 1.9 kilometres, it was used by 60,000 vehicles daily in 1996. In the distance, the Hong Kong Golf Club's 9-hole course at Deep Water Bay can be seen on the left above the beach. To the right are the inviting pools of Waterworld, from which the Ocean Park cablecar climbs the headland. On the other side of Deep Water Bay is the yacht anchorage at Middle Island.

▌Right
Waterworld Next to the lowland section of Ocean Park in Shouson Hill, Waterworld is one of Southeast Asia's most popular water play parks. Each summer, some 300,000 visitors enjoy cooling off in its 4.5 million litres of clear water. Major attractions include the Sea Horse Lagoon, a splash pool featuring slides and diving platforms; the Rapids Ride, an exciting descent negotiated on an inner tube; the Wave Pool with waves one metre high; and Giant Water Slides where riders hurtle down a super-smooth surface, twisting and turning on a tide of water before plunging into a splash pool below.

▌Following pages
Aberdeen, 1982 In the early 1980s, Aberdeen was in the process of full-scale development. High-rise apartments had already been built on the mainland and more would soon follow on the island of Ap Lei Chau opposite, thanks to the bridge which was opened in 1979. The power station on Ap Lei Chau has since been demolished and replaced with a residential development. The fishing junks in the harbour belong to some of the then 35,000 sea-going members of the Tanka and Hoklo peoples; there are rather fewer now. The Aberdeen Marina Club is seen under construction on the left. In front of it, the three famous floating restaurants in the typhoon shelter are still thriving today.

Left
Aberdeen, 1924 Taken during one of the very first aerial photography flights over Hong Kong in 1924, this photograph shows an untouched Aberdeen, then an old fishing town. The shipyards on the waterfront of the island of Ap Lei Chau are a hive of activity and there is a small community of fisherfok living on junks, but no protecting harbour wall has yet been built to create a typhoon shelter. It was from Aberdeen that, in the Ming Dynasty, wood from the incense tree, which flourished in the area around Hong Kong, was loaded into large vessels for shipment to Canton. In the foreground Staunton Creek has now been reduced to a concrete-faced nullah.

Right
Aberdeen Despite recent development, Aberdeen remains home to one of Hong Kong's largest fishing fleets and hundreds of fisherfolk still live on junks in Aberdeen Harbour (right). In contrast, luxury yachts are moored at the Aberdeen Marina Club (foreground) and in the typhoon shelter (left). In the centre are the famous floating restaurants to which customers are taken by special ferry. A bridge links Aberdeen with Ap Lei Chau ("Duck's Tongue Island"). Though increasingly covered with highrise residential developments, the island is still known for its boatyards which line the waterfront, specializing in the building and repair of small craft. A *kaito* (ferry) service operates from Aberdeen to the village of Sok Kwu Wan, famous for its seafood, on Lamma Island (top).

Overleaf
Pokfulam Pokfulam, on the west side of Hong Kong Island, is a quiet, mainly residential area overlooking the east Lamma Channel. The tall white building dominating the photograph is the Queen Mary Hospital, one of the largest government hospitals in Hong Kong, beneath the hill called High West. In front of the light brown high-rise residential development known appropriately as Scenic Villas (right), is the Hong Kong University sports ground. Some of the residential buildings above also belong to the university, although the main campus is further round the island towards Central.

KOWLOON

3625 68I/6 II NOV. 45 // F20 20

Pages 82-83
Tsim Sha Tsui Tsim Sha Tsui means 'sharp sandy point' but reclamation has changed its shape, and beaches are certainly a thing of the past. Instead there are now several 'points' jutting out from the promontory, formed by piers. The *Queen Elizabeth II* lies majestically alongside the Ocean Terminal, Hong Kong's main berth for luxury cruise liners. On the pier behind it, the structure styled like a ship with a white vaulted roof over its deck, is the Pacific Club. Developed by the Hongkong & Kowloon Wharf & Godown Company, this swathe of waterfront is filled by an interconnected complex of international hotels, shopping malls and offices. The famous ferries of the Star Ferry Company provide one of the few remaining links with the last century — they still cross the harbour, as they have done since 1898.

Left and Above
Tsim Sha Tsui, 1997 and 1945 The tip of the Kowloon peninsula has undergone significant changes since the end of the Second World War. As seen in the 1945 photograph, the Kowloon-Canton Railway used to run down the eastern waterfront to its terminus near the Star Ferry pier. In 1975 the Railway terminus moved northeast to Hung Hom, beside the entrance to the first Cross Harbour Tunnel; only its 44-metre clock tower remains today. The Star Ferry has stayed at its original position on the southwest corner of the peninsula, although a new two-pronged pier has replaced the old berth alongside. Meanwhile, the public piers on the west side have been replaced by the Ocean Terminal and China Ferry Terminal. East of the old railway line, extensive reclamation has allowed the creation of the office, hotel and shopping area of Tsim Sha Tsui East.

Left
Tsim Sha Tsui, early 1980s Behind the Star Ferry
pier, the original clock tower stands lonely sentinel in front
of the site of the Kowloon-Canton Railway terminus,
demolished in 1978 to make way for the construction of
the Cultural Centre complex, which would be completed
in 1989. The domed Space Museum already stands
opposite the famous Peninsula, the grand old lady of Hong
Kong hotels, in contrast with the new Regent and New
World hotel and shopping complexes on the waterfront
(right). Behind the Ocean Terminal, the vast Ocean Centre
and Harbour City development stretches along the
western edge of the peninsula. The residential blocks there
have since been demolished to make way for further
commercial development. In the background the Kai Tak
runway extends into the harbour beneath the Anderson
Road Quarry.

Above
Canton Road Flanked by Canton Road and Kowloon Park Drive, the low, white Marine Police Headquarters building, screened on three sides by shrubbery, harks back to a colonial past. In the bottom right-hand corner, the Salisbury YMCA, with its location at the heart of Tsim Sha Tsui, is a popular hostelry complete with swimming pool, squash courts and health centre. Just visible on the left of Canton Road are the waterfront Ocean Terminal, Star House and Ocean Centre.

Right
West Kowloon Reclamation Work began in 1990 to create 340 hectares of new land between Yaumati and Lai Chi Kok, and by March 1998, infrastructure to serve the new airport was nearing completion. In the foreground is the entrance to Western Harbour Crossing road tunnel, while beyond it, the Kowloon terminus of the Airport Railway is under construction. The *Queen Elizabeth II* cruise liner can be seen berthed at Ocean Terminal, jutting out from the Tsim Sha Tsui peninsula, with the north shore of Hong Kong Island in the distance.

■ Above

Salisbury Road Facing Salisbury Road, Kowloon's grand old hotel, the Peninsula, has been expanded by a new tower, constructed after the building height restriction for this area was lifted. The dramatic range of hills in the background is the legendary source of Kowloon's name, which means 'nine dragons' — one for each of the eight peaks and a ninth in deference to the Song emperor, who established a temporary court here in the 13th century.

■ Right

The Harbour Hong Kong's most prized natural asset, its deepwater harbour, is crisscrossed by ferries and lighters all day long. 'Kowloon side' and 'Hong Kong side' are the local terms for the two parts of the city separated by this watery divide. While Hong Kong Island was acquired by the British in 1841, the Kowloon peninsula was not ceded until 1860. For years Kowloon was considered slightly disreputable, possibly because, after it was settled, it was the site of a naval yard, military camp, and countless gambling houses. More recently, it has become literally true that the inhabitants of Hong Kong, living in ever taller apartment blocks in the Mid-Levels or the Peak, can 'look down' on the denizens of Kowloon.

Top left
Space Museum Opened in 1980, this complex consists of an auditorium, exhibition and lecture halls, and a bookshop. Highly advanced audiovisual equipment is used to describe and explain the mysteries of astronomy and the achievements of space explorers. Salisbury Garden to its right has been laid out above an underground shopping and parking complex.

Bottom left
New World Centre Looking down on the rooftop swimming pools of the Regent Hotel (left) and the New World Hotel (right). The shopping arcades of the New World Centre are conveniently next door.

Right
Tsim Sha Tsui From the tip of the peninsula protruding into the harbour, the Kowloon shoreline on the west is being dramatically altered by the massive landfill project which includes Stonecutters Island in its sweep. The western point of Hong Kong island is just visible on the left.

Left
Tsim Sha Tsui East Around the freight terminal (foreground) are the lighters, fitted with cranes, which carry out mid-stream unloading of containers. From here the freight is transferred to trains bound for mainland China. This is a rare view of a relatively empty entrance to the Cross Harbour Tunnel (upper right), for once not clogged with traffic.

Right
Hung Hom Behind the freight terminal, sitting on a raised podium, is the square grey roof of the Hong Kong Coliseum. Built over the railway terminus, this functional-looking stadium seats 12,500 spectators under cover and has played host to international orchestras as well as sporting events. Reclamation at Hung Hom Bay, now complete, will enable the Kowloon-Canton Railway to extend its freight yard and provide land for residential and industrial use. Whampoa Gardens and Whampoa Estates (foreground) are residential complexes built over old dockyards. The swimming pools are open to the public.

Top left
Kowloon Bay Overlooked by the oddly shaped
peak known as Lion Rock (upper right), Kowloon Bay is an
industrial area characterised by its low-rise roofline, the
result of an official building height restriction imposed to
ensure safe aircraft approaches to Kai Tak airport. When
the airport is relocated to Chek Lap Kok, this area will be
totally transformed by a development plan which includes
further reclamation of the bay, new highways and large-
scale urban restructuring. The low buildings with the blue
roofs house a sewage treatment plant.

Bottom left
Kai Tak Hong Kong's international airport, named
after the two men who brought it into being in 1928, is
one of the busiest transport hubs in the world. When it
first opened, the aerodrome had a grass landing strip and
a series of matsheds either side of a noxious nullah. Its
present runway, protruding into the harbour, was
constructed in the 1950s by French engineers.

Right
Kai Tak An unusual shot showing one landed plane
taxiing on the runway, and another taking off. More than
400 aircraft — or one every two minutes at peak periods
— arrive or depart every day. Virtually the whole of Hong
Kong's north shore is clearly caught in the view. The white
cruisers in the harbour on the right are gambling ships
which pick up passengers in the evening, sail into
international waters, and return the following morning
when the punters disembark.

▌Above

Hong Kong Island and Kowloon, c. 1990 When this photograph was taken, the decision to build Hong Kong's new airport at Chek Lap Kok had just been made, and plans were already afoot for the complicated transport network which would be necessary for access. In one of the most ambitious civil engineering projects in history, a new harbour crossing would connect with an expressway, to be built on reclaimed land west of the existing peninsula, and thence via a series of bridges, viaducts and expressways to Lantau. In this picture, the reclamation has barely started and Stonecutters Island is still an island, whereas today it is joined to the mainland by Terminal 8 of the Kwai Chung Container Terminal.

▌Right

West Kowloon Reclamation Although well advanced, the reclamation shows little more than a complicated network of roads at present. In front of the blue and yellow ventilation shaft of the Western Harbour Crossing is the entrance to the tunnel, the third to connect the island to the mainland. Other transport links, all to be developed as part of the new airport programme, will include the Airport Railway (its depot is being built to the left of the tunnel entrance), a mass transit service, and the West Kowloon Expressway. With its southern terminus on Hong Kong Island, the railway track will run under the harbour.

Left
Kowloon Tong In 1860 the peninsula of Kowloon up to an east-west line demarcated by today's Boundary Street and just enclosing the area occupied by Kai Tak was added to the British colony of Hong Kong. North of Boundary Street sprawls a residential and industrial zone encompassing Kowloon Tong, characterised by pleasant low-rise housing along tree-lined roads (centre of the picture), and extending to the Lion Rock Tunnel entrance (bottom right-hand corner). Across the harbour from the western side of the peninsula, where reclamation work is under way, the waterfront of Hong Kong Island appears very close.

Above
West Kowloon Expressway Running from Lai Chi Kok to the Western Harbour Crossing, this expressway connects with a section of elevated road on the west of Hong Kong Island and is designed to be a component of a fast road link to the airport at Chek Lap Kok. Also on the west of the peninsula is the Kwai Chung container port, the busiest in the world. Eight terminals now extend as far as Stonecutters Island, cutting off the four-metre channel that previously separated it from the mainland.

Following page
Stonecutters Island Seen from the helicopter cockpit, Stonecutters Island is now incorporated into the mainland, since the attachment of Terminal 8 of the Kwai Chung container port. It also provides a naval base for the Chinese garrison stationed in Hong Kong since the territory became a Special Administrative Region of China on July 1, 1997. This modern role is in contrast with the past: for decades Stonecutters Island accommodated only an off-limits military depot and provided a congenial environment for such creatures as nesting kites, pythons, fish-eating cormorants and even the rarely seen hoopoe. With development, the future for its wildlife is less rosy.

NEW TERRITORIES

Shipping Hong Kong's perfect natural harbour and its shipping remain the territory's lifeblood. Every year Hong Kong plays host to an amazing number and variety of craft.

Clockwise from top left:

• A sleek cruise liner leaves the Ocean Terminal. Behind it, a Star Ferry dodges a tug towing a vessel through the harbour.

• A container vessel leaves Hong Kong.

• Another container ship prepares to dock at Kwai Chung Container Port.

• Lighters in the Yau Ma Tei typhoon shelter help to offload cargoes from vessels moored in the harbour.

• Powerboats are sometimes used for smuggling between Hong Kong and the mainland.

• Behind a brightly coloured freighter lying at a mooring buoy, a coastal vessel crosses in front of a lighter being towed into harbour, an outlying islands ferry and a high speed ferry to Macau.

• Tugs tow sections of the new Western Harbour Tunnel across the harbour to be lowered into place.

▌Left
Lai Chi Kok Pulling away from Stonecutters Island, the helicopter hovers over Lai Chi Kok, a densely populated light industrial and residential area of Kowloon. This section of the new expressway provides greatly enhanced access to the container port, seen in the background.

▌Above
Stonecutters Island Terminal 8 is a patchwork of strong colours contrasting starkly with the greenery which still covers much of the island. As seaborne traffic through Hong Kong continues to increase, heavy demands are made on the port's handling capacity and efficiency. This terminal is the newest, but the development of Terminals 9, 10 and 11 are already in progress. Much in evidence in this shot are the lighters which contribute to the efficiency of the port. They move cargo at mid-stream between ships at mooring buoys and handling areas on shore. The vessel in front is, however, not a workboat but one of the ferries plying the route to Tuen Mun in the northwest.

Previous pages
Kwai Chung Terminals 6 and 7, with the quay-side gantry cranes and serried rows of containers, are shown here in close-up. Annual cargo-handling reached an astonishing 13.4 million TEUs or 20-foot equivalent units in 1996. Hong Kong was colonised in 1841 to facilitate trade with China; and trade, particularly the re-export and transshipment of goods to international destinations, remains the territory's lifeblood.

Above
Stonecutters Island Containers are being discharged from two ships at Terminal 8 by huge gantry cranes. The average ship turn-around time is an amazing twelve hours. Much of the process of loading, unloading and storage of containers — which are all exactly the same size — is carried out by sophisticated automation. Hong Kong's port is, uniquely, not controlled by a port authority. The eight container terminals at Kwai Chung and Stonecutters have been developed entirely by the private sector.

Right
Kwai Chung Modern Terminals Limited (which occupies the building on the far left, under the bend of the elevated road), Sealand Orient (grey building) and Hong Kong International Terminals (blue and white building) are among the major operators of container terminals at Kwai Chung.

▌Above
Tsing Yi and Kwai Chung Tsing Yi Island
(foreground), separated from the mainland of Kowloon by
a narrow channel, is one of two 'stepping stones' to the
new Chek Lap Kok airport on Lantau. This view shows
two new bridges, one road and one rail, sweeping up from
west Kowloon, over Kwai Chung, and across the Rambler
Channel.

▌Right
Tsing Yi, c. 1982 In the early 1980s, the only link
from Tsing Yi to Kowloon was via a single road bridge,
which created serious congestion getting onto or leaving
the island. Now there are not only two road bridges at
this location, but also another road bridge further north
and a railway bridge leading to Chek Lap Kok. The other
major difference is the extent of container port
development at Kwai Chung (centre, top).

Above
Tsing Yi Over the green hills, on the island's west and south, is an industrial area with oil depots, ship repair yards, and facilities for building and servicing oil rigs. The ship under repair here is in a floating dry-dock.

Right
Lantau Link The need to provide easy access to the new airport on the north side of Lantau Island has meant several huge and complicated transportation projects including the construction of two bridges. Tsing Yi, the first stepping stone from the mainland, is joined to Ma Wan, another island and the second stepping stone. From a viaduct over Ma Wan a second bridge in turn spans Kap Shui Mun to Lantau. The Tsing Ma suspension bridge is seen here from just above the Shell depot on Tsing Yi. The pedestrians on the expressway (bottom right) were participating in a 'Walk for Millions', an event not only to raise funds for local charities but also, in this case, to mark the opening of the Lantau Link.

▌Left
Kap Shui Mun Bridge While the Tsing Ma is the longest road and rail traffic suspension bridge in the world, a shorter span joins the small island of Ma Wan to Lantau (foreground).

▌Above
Tsing Yi The length of the island is captured here, with the Tsing Ma Bridge on the north and the industrial area on the south.

█ Left
Ting Kau Bridge The bridge had not quite edged out over the water when this view was shot in early 1997. Planned to connect with Route 3 at Castle Peak, it will carry traffic to the northwest New Territories and beyond to southern China.

█ Above
Tsing Ma Bridge Opened by Baroness Thatcher in April 1997, the Lantau Link, comprising the Tsing Ma Bridge, the Ma Wan viaduct and the Kap Shui Mun Bridge, is now an impressive Hong Kong landmark. With pylons over 200 metres high and a main span of 1,377 metres, the Tsing Ma is the world's longest suspension bridge carrying both road and rail traffic. The bridge deck is 62 metres above sea level, enabling ocean-going ships to continue to use the busy Rambler Channel. On the horizon are the islands of Hong Kong and Lamma.

■ Left
Ting Kau Bridge In October 1996, when this picture was taken, the span of the bridge was still only demarcated by its pylons. On the right, the traffic jam seen at Castle Peak is a telling vindication of the extensive road construction programme. Since the early 1980s, when many Hong Kong companies relocated their manufacturing and processing operations to southern China's special economic zones, cross-border traffic has expanded dramatically. Entry and exit formalities at the border are still required although Hong Kong has reverted to Chinese rule. The Ting Kau Bridge and road network from Castle Peak to the border will considerably relieve the congestion.

■ Above
Ting Kau Bridge This graceful bridge, connects Tsing Yi Island with the northwest New Territories, providing a more direct route to the Mainland.

Left
Tuen Mun, c.1982 In the 1970s and 1980s, the rural hinterland of the New Territories was transformed by the establishment of several new towns designed to provide work and housing for thousands of families. One of the first of these, Tuen Mun, in the northwest New Territories, was built largely on land reclaimed from Castle Peak Bay. Development proceeded on either side of a large nullah which is all that remains of a river that once flowed into the bay. Tuen Mun means "garrison entrance", a reflection of its historical importance as a military port in the Tang Dynasty (618-907 AD). Castle Peak is on the left; the Tai Lam Hills on the right.

Above
Tuen Mun, 1997 Mixed housing and light industrial development have changed Tuen Mun beyond recognition in recent years. Today over 400,000 people live in the town, many of them in fancifully named high-rise developments like Butterfly Estates, Melody Garden and Miami Beach Towers. An example of these developments can be seen in the foreground of this picture; the Gold Coast is directly across the bay. Due to inadequate road and rail links to the northwest New Territories, many commuters rely on a high-speed hover ferry service operating from the pier in the foreground.

Left
West New Territories Population density, rapid economic development and urbanisation, and lack of public awareness pose a constant challenge to those involved in protecting the environment in Hong Kong. Proper disposal of solid waste which avoids the production of polluting liquids and gases is a part of the drive to contain environmental problems. Most solid waste is transferred to landfills in unpopulated areas in the New Territories, such as this one.

Above
Deep Bay Beyond the landfill, a bay separates the northwest New Territories from the Special Economic Zone of Shenzhen in Guangdong. On the right, the protruding towers of housing estates pinpoint the location of Tin Shui Wai, another new town being developed, mainly by private enterprise, in the wake of improved transport provisions. The town's proximity to the border with the mainland is also expected to fuel its expansion.

Above
Mai Po Marshes, early 1980s The sun sets over the Mai Po Marshes, Hong Kong's one remaining wetland of any size, and Shekou in the distance. The present-day marshes were originally a mangrove swamp along Deep Bay in the northwest New Territories. In the 1940s a bund was built along the seaward edge and the land it enclosed was cleared and divided into fish ponds. Much of the area has since been drained to provide land for housing, but the marshes are still an important staging post for thousands of migratory birds. The area is run as a nature reserve by the World Wide Fund for Nature.

Right
Shekou From Deep Bay, the modern face of Shekou spreads out and extends all the way round the coast to Shenzhen. China's economic reform programme was spearheaded by an export-processing zone at Shekou, set up in 1979, and four special economic zones — Shantou, Shenzhen, Zhuhai and Xiamen — established in 1980. Designed to attract foreign investment by offering infrastructure, factory premises, plentiful labour and tax breaks, the zones allowed Hong Kong manufacturers, always constrained by land shortage, to shift their production to the mainland.

▌Above
Yuen Long Sited south of an expanse of fish and shrimp ponds on the eastern edge of Deep Bay, Yuen Long town burgeoned in the 1970s. The first settlement of this area, by Hakka clans from southern China, can be traced back to the 11th century. To the right of the urban core is the Yuen Long Industrial Estate. On the right of the frame is Tin Shui Wai.

▌Right
Lau Fau Shan 'Shan' means mountains, but to all appearances Lau Fau Shan sits on rather flat, marshy land, and the only 'mountains' here are those of discarded oyster shells extending ever further into Deep Bay. Immediately west of Tin Shui Wai and south of mainland China across the bay, Lau Fau Shan is a fishing village which specialises in oysters and other seafood. The oysters are dried or made into oyster sauce. Stacked containers are now familiar eyesores in the New Territories.

▌ Above
Yuen Long Industrial Estate Providing
employment for a large proportion of the local population,
this industrial estate offers competitively-priced premises
to businesses with operations which cannot be efficiently
carried out in multi-storey factories. A sewage treatment
plant can be seen to its left.

▌ Right
Yuen Long and Tuen Mun, c. 1989 Taken from
near the border with the mainland, looking southwest, this
photograph shows a typical New Territories landscape of
rolling hills interspersed with uncontrolled development.
Beyond the fishponds of Lau Fau Shan are the new towns
of Yuen Long (top, centre) and Tuen Mun beneath the
sharp point of Castle Peak. The mountains of Lantau Island
tower in the background, at this date showing no signs of
the airport development to follow.

■ Left
Kwai Tau Leng The northeastern New Territories is one of the few remaining areas of Hong Kong where vegetable cultivation takes place. This kind of idyllic rural scene is now rare, as most agricultural land has either been abandoned by families who have moved elsewhere, or blighted by container storage or vehicle breakers' yards. Most vegetables consumed in Hong Kong today are imported from the mainland. Behind the traditional village houses, burial sites are carefully chosen for their auspicious location on the hillside.

■ Above
Fairview Park Continuing transformation of the environment is represented by these sprawling residential estates built on the fringes of the protected Mai Po Marshes Nature Reserve. They are the middle-class housing developments of Fairview Park on the left and Palm Springs in the foreground.

Above and right
Mai Po Marshes The Mai Po Marshes are shown on many maps as a large stretch of ponds in the northwest corner of the New Territories. Actually many of the ponds are commercial fish and prawn farms, and the Mai Po Marshes Nature Reserve occupies a clearly defined, 380-hectare wetland of mangrove, mudflats and ponds to the left of Fairview Park. Deep Bay is on the flight path of thousands of migratory birds which stop to feed on the mudflats twice a year. Over 270 species of birds, several of them quite rare, have been sighted here. In the distance lies Shenzhen, behind the river that defines the border.

Left
Fairview Park Although farmlands in the New Territories are fast shrinking, the residents of this enclave, as well as those of Palm Springs (left), are still able to look out over fields and ponds. Lam Tsuen Peak rises behind, while Tai Mo Shan, the highest point in Hong Kong, dominates the centre of the dark range on the horizon.

Above
Wo Shang Wai Perched on a tiny islet in the middle of the Mai Po Marshes, this village is surrounded by water. This shot appeared in the first volume of *Over Hong Kong*, published in 1982. The village did not sell out to the developers of Palm Springs and clings on to existence, engulfed almost entirely by the new complex. It can just be seen in the shot opposite, hard against the left edge, squeezed between two triangular-shaped plots.

Left and above
Northern New Territories Urbanisation is eating away farmland and these villages, no more than clusters of squat whitewashed houses roofed in grey tiles, are also beleaguered. Containers encroach everywhere; it is doubtful if the unspoilt village hugging the hillside (above) will long escape the blight.

Right
Northern New Territories Walled villages, a feature of the New Territories, were built several centuries ago when the first settlers needed to protect themselves from bandits and other immigrants. The walls and some traditional grey houses can still be seen in this shot, although a preference for Spanish-style villas has now made the village something of an architectural hotchpotch.

▌Left
Sha Tau Kok Perched above Starling Inlet, Sha Tau Kok is right on the border with mainland China. The border crossing is delineated by the low buildings with flat grey roofs at the top of the road, just below the high-rises which are on the mainland side.

▌Above
Plover Cove Wong Leng, the peak in the foreground, towers 639 metres above the Plover Cove Reservoir, a water catchment area in Tolo Harbour. Despite the presence of many large reservoirs and abundant rainfall, Hong Kong is not self-sufficient in water, and supplies need to be supplemented by 720 million cubic metres piped from Guangdong Province every year.

Left
Tolo Harbour Famed for its pearl fisheries in the centuries before British rule, this natural harbour is set in a beautiful landscape typically dominated by scrub-covered hills plunging into the sparkling blue sea. The barrage marks the division between the harbour and the Plover Cove Reservoir.

Above
Tai Po Industrial Estate Over the last 20 years, Hong Kong's economy has moved away from manufacturing towards the provision of services. Nevertheless, the territory is still keen to attract high-tech industries. Factory space for such enterprises is provided at cost by the Hong Kong Industrial Estates Corporation. This picture shows the first estate to be built, at Tai Po, in the northeast New Territories.

▋Above

Tai Po The site of a famous market on the western end of Tolo Harbour, Tai Po has burgeoned along with other new towns. In the early 1980s, when this shot was taken, it had a population of some 25,000; now it supports more than a quarter of a million inhabitants.

▋Right

Tai Po Government development of new towns was seen as a way of relieving population density in urban areas and coping with Hong Kong's housing shortage. Today more than half of Hong Kong's people live in subsidised accommodation, 2.9 million of them in the New Territories in towns such as Tai Po.

Left
Tai Po This shot captures the town from further away, and reveals Ma On Shan on the right-hand side of Tolo Harbour. Snaking between the apartment towers is the track of the Kowloon-Canton Railway (left), which provides a commuter service for the new towns in the New Territories and, as its name implies, carries passengers and freight across the border.

Above
Tolo Highway A new housing development is being constructed above this stretch of the Tolo Highway with the Kowloon-Canton railroad beside it. The Tolo Highway carries traffic speedily from Tai Po to Shatin. Just ahead, on top of the hill just where the highway disappears to the right, are the buildings of the Chinese University of Hong Kong. Founded in 1963, the university has over 10,000 students.

▌Left
Shatin This shot, taken from about 4,000 feet above Shatin in the late 1970s, shows the race track under construction. Hong Kong's racing scene is renowned for the huge sums wagered at every meeting. This second racecourse, which alternates with the older, Happy Valley one, was completed in 1978. It encloses a landscaped park which can be visited on non-racing days.

▌Above
Shatin A reverse angle shot of the same site shown on the previous page, this was taken from a lower altitude. On the left is the Shing Mun Channel, once a naturally flowing river debouching into Tolo Harbour. Today the new town of Shatin, home to more than half a million people, shows no hint of its origin as a sandy cove dotted with villages. The sewage treatment works (foreground) are situated next to the Hong Kong Jockey Club's stables. Behind them are the racecourse and stands. The video screens on the side of the track in front of the stands come alive on race days with close-ups of horses and jockeys, slow-motion replays of the action and information on the changing odds.

Left
Shatin and Ma On Shan Ma On Shan viewed from above Shatin, which is to its southeast, looks just what it is: an unfinished new town. Tucked into the narrow strip of coast at the foot of Hong Kong's highest point, Ma On Shan town has been created by private developers on the south side of Tolo Harbour. Shatin with its sewage treatment works overlooked by luxury residential developments fills the foreground.

Above
Ma On Shan In 1993 a 'Sandwich Class Housing Scheme' was introduced to help middle-income families to buy their own homes. This involves loans to applicants on favourable terms as well as sales of property at a discount. Several developments at Ma On Shan were constructed under this scheme.

Right
Clearwater Bay On a peninsula south of Sai Kung, the Clearwater Bay Country Club with its golf course and marina is a beautifully sited private recreation centre. The humps looming out of the sea directly opposite the clubhouse are the group of islands known as the Ninepins.

Overleaf
Kau Sai Chau An island facing Sai Kung across Port Shelter, Kau Sai Chau used to be a firing range for the army. It is now chiefly visited because it has Hong Kong's only public golf course. Designed by Gary Player and funded by the Hong Kong Jockey Club, the course has 27 holes; the championship North Course is reckoned to be amongst the best and most challenging in Southeast Asia. Kau Sai Chau is reached by ferry from Sai Kung.

OUTLYING ISLANDS

| Above

Tsing Ma Bridge The amazing engineering feat of the Lantau Link, which is double-decked to carry both a road and a railway, is made up of this bridge, the viaduct over Ma Wan, and the Kap Shui Mun Bridge. Tsing Ma is a sight to behold: larger than San Francisco's famed Golden Gate Bridge, it has a span of 1,377 metres, and its pylons are 206 metres high.

| Right

Tsing Ma Bridge A day of celebration (11 May 1997) is captured in this shot, when thousands of proud Hong Kong citizens donned their tracksuits and took to the roads in a 'Walk for Millions' to mark the opening of the Lantau Link. The bridge itself was officially inaugurated a month earlier by Baroness Thatcher.

▌Left
North Lantau Expressway Part of the transport system associated with the Chek Lap Kok airport opens up north Lantau, a measure which dismays environmental conservationists but promises huge economic benefits to the land-hungry community. Sections of the North Lantau Expressway, a six-lane, 12.5-kilometre road, as well as the railway depot seen on the left, are built on reclaimed land. Just visible in the distant haze are Kowloon to the left and Hong Kong Island to the right.

▌Above
Chek Lap Kok and Tung Chung, c. 1990
The challenge for the developers of Hong Kong's new airport is to preserve as far as possible the tranquillity of Lantau, while still catering for the needs of one of the world's busiest international airports. This picture shows Chek Lap Kok as a peaceful island and the Tung Chung valley before its development into a new town. It will be interesting to see whether development pressures can be resisted for the rest of Lantau.

Left

Hong Kong International Airport The airport site has been created by the levelling of an island, Chek Lap Kok, off the north shore of Lantau, and extensive landfill. Although the need for a new airport to replace the overstretched Kai Tak had long been recognised, the Chek Lap Kok project, with its stupendous price tag, was highly controversial. The decision was made in 1989; as the project would straddle the transfer of sovereignty in July 1997, China was consulted, but the negotiations became caught up in disputes between Britain and China over political reforms in Hong Kong. Site preparation work advanced despite lack of agreement on a number of key issues. From an earlier forecast of June 1997, the airport opening date was postponed to mid-1998.

Top right

Chek Lap Kok Featuring a spectacular gull-wing vaulted and cantilevered roof, a design to ensure efficient energy insulation, the passenger terminal building is on the northeast side of the reclamation. A view of Tuen Mun is afforded by its panoramic windows. Inside the central concourse, two kilometres of moving walkways and an automated driverless train move passengers to and from their planes. The vivid green patch at the bottom of the frame represents a victory for conservationists: it is the habitat of the Romer's tree frog.

Bottom right

The Brothers Two islands known as The Brothers have been flattened to remove a potential obstruction to low-flying aircraft and for landfill.

Above
Chek Lap Kok Runway A milestone in Hong Kong's aviation history was reached on 20 February 1997, when the first landing by a fixed-wing, Government Flying Service aircraft was made at Chek Lap Kok. Air traffic is expected to grow apace, and this runway will be supplemented by a second one, to be built on the northern seaward side of the site, by the end of the century.

Left
Chek Lap Kok The miniature vehicles along the rim of the reclamation provide scale to the massive size of the airport runway.

Right
Tung Chung New Town Designed to house a population of 200,000 by the year 2011, the new town of Tung Chung is being developed primarily as an airport support community.

Opposite page
Chek Lap Kok The terminal's Y-shaped central concourse has 38 airbridge gates connecting aircraft to the building. Apart from the road, the shore opposite still looks pristine — for the moment. This is merely the lull before the storm, however.

▍Above
Lantau A deHavilland Tiger Moth over northeast
Lantau in the early 1980s, when construction of the
Discovery Bay complex was still at the site preparation
stage. The Tiger Moth was built in 1941 and restored to its
original state by a Captain Dave Baker in 1976. It was
flown for pleasure and kept in the New Territories before
Captain Baker moved it to a new home in Australia.

▍Right
Discovery Bay This offshore residential and resort
complex offers a car-free environment, though its denizens
are often to be seen taking the shopping home in golf carts.
The carts' proper setting is the 18-hole hilltop golf course in
the foreground. Peng Chau rises out of the sea at upper
right. A hovercraft speeds away from the pier (left) on its
frequent service to Central District, Hong Kong Island.

Above
Kwun Yum Temple This temple tucked away on a secluded hillside in southeast Lantau was restored by Hong Kong tycoon, Li Ka-shing, and dedicated to the memory of his wife. Kwun Yum or the Goddess of Mercy is a Buddhist deity. A much more modest shrine stood there before, on a site granted by Sir Cecil Clementi (Governor of Hong Kong, 1925-30) to a loyal servant.

Right
Po Lin Monastery Chinese temples and monasteries were traditionally established in remote and tranquil places, and this one, on the Ngong Ping plateau, southwest Lantau, is no exception. On holidays and at weekends, though, it throngs with visitors. Its name means 'Precious Lotus', the lotus being a Buddhist symbol of the belief that salvation or Nirvana is possible for all. The 26-metre-high Temple of Heaven Buddha, glittering in bronze, looks benignly upon the scene.

▍Preceding pages
Giant Buddha Evening sun falls on the great Buddha, his hand raised in benediction, above the Po Lin Monastery on Lantau Island. The 26-metre Buddha, which sits on a lotus throne on top of a three-platform altar and weighs 202 tonnes, is the world's largest seated, outdoor, bronze Buddha. Built in 1990 to face China, on a clear day it can be seen from as far away as Macau. Visitors can walk up the 268 steps to the statue.

▍Left and above
Cheung Chau Now and then — Lantau's much smaller neighbour has a fishing community and is distinctive for its seafood restaurants and lively atmosphere. It was very much a haunt of pirates and smugglers in the old days; now its residents are more likely to be office workers commuting daily to Hong Kong Island. Development has accelerated in recent years, as a comparison with Cheung Chau in the early 1950s (above) with its fleet of fishing junks strikingly demonstrates. (Courtesy Russell Spurr)

▍page 172
Lantau Peak Above the Po Lin Monastery, Lantau Peak soars 934 metres above sea level, making it Hong Kong's second highest mountain. In contrast with the man-made landscape on the north shore of Lantau Island, the pristine beauty of Lantau Peak and the surrounding Lantau Country Park still provide miles of unspoilt trails for energetic hikers and nature lovers. On the rare days when it is not shrouded in mist, the summit of Lantau Peak commands a spectacular view over the island.

INDEX

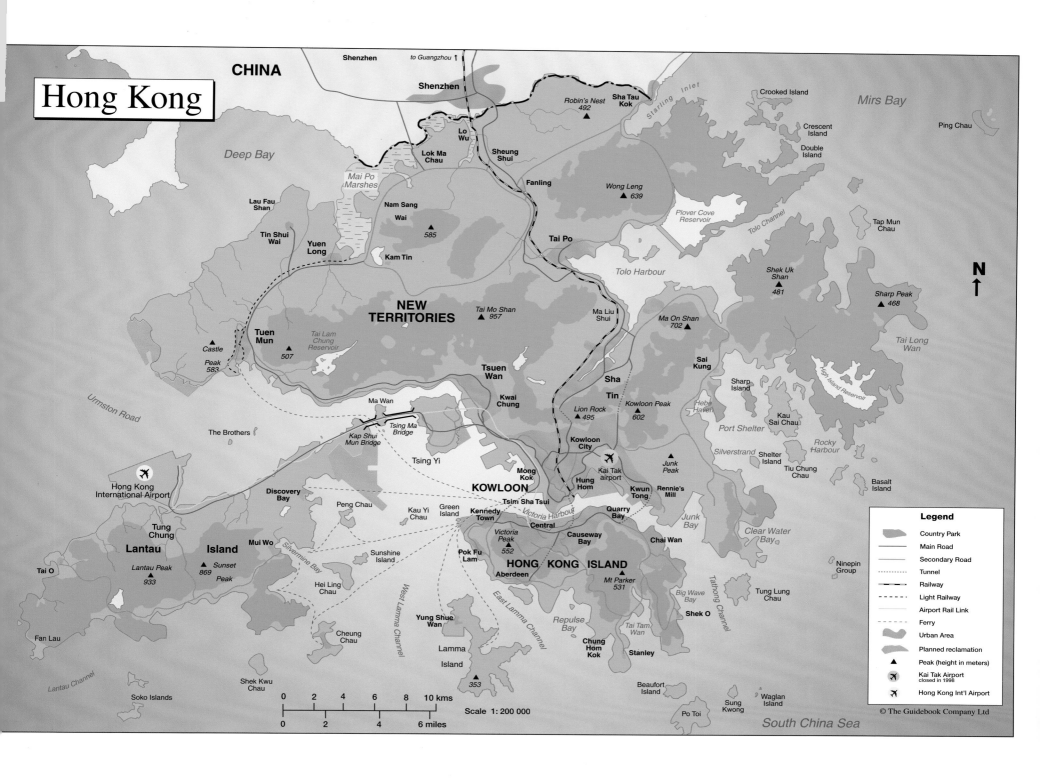